Journey through the Wilderness

A Mindfulness Approach
to the Ancient Jewish Practice
of Counting the Omer

A WAY IN

Rabbi Yael Levy

Journey through the Wilderness
A Mindfulness Approach
to the Ancient Jewish Practice
of Counting the Omer
Fourth Edition

A PROJECT OF

A WAY IN
Philadelphia PA

www.awayin.org
facebook.com/jmindfulness

ISBN - 13: 978-1470083229
ISBN - 10: 1470083221

1. Mindfulness 2. Judaism 3. Prayer 4. Psalms
5. Kabbalah 6. Mysticism 7. Omer 8. Counting the Omer
9. Jewish Mindfulness 10. Spiritual Journey 11. Spirituality

Table of Contents

> *Teach us to count our days, that we may cultivate a heart of wisdom.* — Psalm 90:12

IT WAS A BEAUTIFUL SPRING NIGHT in northern California almost 30 years ago. As our seder on the second night of Passover came to a close, our host invited us out onto his redwood deck. There, under the full moon, he offered thanks, blessed the moment and said, "Today is the first day of the *Omer*."

I had heard the word before but didn't know much beyond that. "What is the *Omer*?" I asked.

Counting the *Omer* is a secret treasure of Jewish tradition, said my friend. It reminds us to count each day, and to make each day count. It guides us on a journey of the spirit, helping us cultivate awareness, discernment and gratitude. "Start counting," he said, "and you will begin to understand."

Despite my host's invitation that night, I did not take on Counting the *Omer* as a spiritual practice until, several years later, I was living in Israel and actively looking for ways to connect to the mystical in Jewish tradition. I was searching for something in Judaism that would be a link to the mystery, something that was beyond rationality. The *Omer* touched into that need. Like many people beginning this practice, my counting was not perfect. Sometimes I forgot; sometimes I lost my place. The *Omer* continued to be intriguing, and each year I found myself looking forward to the *Omer's* challenges and invitations.

Many years later in 2003, my practice of Counting the *Omer* deepened during a month alone in the red rock desert of southern Utah. Each night as three stars appeared in the deep blue sky, I said the prayer and counted the day. Then in the morning, I sat with the qualities of the day and followed their direction, taking notice of the thoughts and emotions that arose and how the qualities felt in my body. Every day, I would record my reflections and discoveries in my journal. In the years since, this *Omer* practice has become my very deep guide.

The next year, I shared the *Omer* with members of my congregation, Mishkan Shalom in Philadelphia, teaching an introductory class and e-mailing *kavannot* — intentions — for each day. Many members of my community were surprised that this practice was part of Judaism. They were attracted by its many different layers, from simple counting without embellishment to entry into the complicated system of the *sefirot* as developed by the Kabbalists.

After many years of exploration, I discovered that Counting the *Omer* was a Mindfulness practice. Counting helps us pay attention, focus on the moment and watch how everything passes. In their directions for counting, the mystics teach us not to say out loud the number of the day that is to come. We are to stay present in the day that is until the very last moment. Then, when each day turns to night, we are to let go fully of what was and step forward into what will be.

Over the past few years, some participants have found support and greater meaning in being part of a spiritual community that shares its experiences of counting. Some people have formed *hevruta* (partnerships), counting on the phone together. Others share their insights via the Internet. In that spirit, we invite you to share your experiences on our Facebook page: facebook.com/jmindfulness.

As my host said many years ago, start counting and you will begin to understand. May the journey be for blessing.

—Rabbi Yael Levy
Philadelphia, Pennsylvania
March 6, 2017
8 Adar 5777

— v —

THE **Q**UALITIES for each day of the Omer are drawn from the lower seven of 10 *sefirot* — attributes of reality as conceived by the Jewish mystics. The *sefirot* are represented as the Tree of Life.

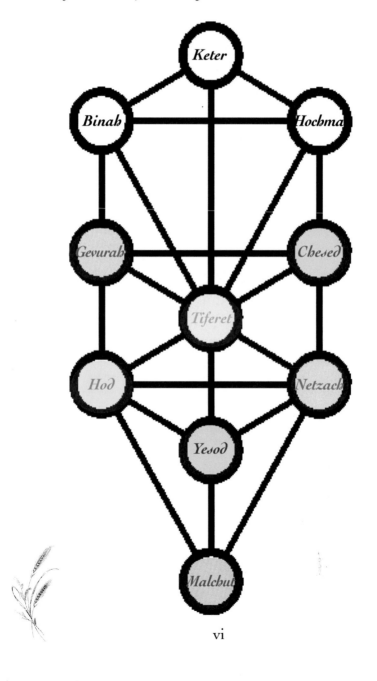

THE COUNTING OF THE *OMER* is the ancient Jewish ritual of blessing and counting each of the 49 days between Passover and *Shavuot*.

The counting began as an agricultural ritual. Our ancestors would pray for an abundant spring harvest by waving a sheaf, an *Omer*, of barley toward the night sky. Over time, this agricultural rite was replaced by liturgy and the counting became the way to mark the Israelites' journey from bondage in Egypt to revelation at Mount Sinai.

For the Kabbalists, the Jewish mystics of the 16th and 17th centuries, the Counting of the *Omer* became a time of spiritual exploration and

cleansing, a way for us to prepare our souls to receive the divine guidance that comes to us each year on *Shavuot*.

Counting the *Omer* is a 49-day mindfulness practice aimed at helping us pay attention to the movement of our lives, to notice the subtle shifts, the big changes, the yearnings, the strivings, the disappointments, the fears, hopes and joys. It is an opportunity for deep introspection, a call to notice our inclinations, our default responses, our reactions to shifting emotions and circumstances. The *Counting of the Omer* seeks to cleanse and renew our *nefesh, ruach* and *neshamah* (layers of body, mind and soul) so we can respond to the circumstances of our lives with compassion and wisdom.

The mystical tradition teaches that these 49 days between Passover and *Shavuot* are divided into seven-week periods, with each week containing a specific spiritual quality. The qualities are guided by seven of the ten *sefirot*, the Divine emanations through which, the mystics believed, God reveals Godself in the world.

WEEKS OF THE OMER

Week One
Chesed — Generosity, Love, Compassion

Week Two
Gevurah — Strength, Judgment, Discernment

Week Three
Tiferet — Radiance, Harmony, Balance, Truth

Week Four
Netzach — Eternity, Vision, Endurance

Week Five
Hod — Presence, Gratitude

Week Six
Yesod — Foundation, Connection

Week Seven
Malchut/Shechina — Majesty, Divine Presence

On each of the 49 days, two of the qualities intersect with each other so that each day is unique.

The invitation is to count each day and, as we do, to meditate and reflect on the spiritual qualities. Week by week, day by day, let these qualities focus our attention, pose questions and challenge our perceptions.

The Israelites' journey took place in the vastness of the desert where they encountered their deepest fears and their most expansive visions. It was in that desert that they heard the Divine speak, instructing them how to live in relationship to themselves and all creation with awe, reverence and gratitude.

The Hebrew word for "desert wilderness" – *midbar* — is the same word for "speak," *midaber*. The mystics teach that when we leave our routines, habits and expectations and allow ourselves to go into the unknown—to traverse the wilderness of mind and spirit—we open ourselves to receive Divine guidance. *"God midaber in the midbar."* The Divine speaks in the wilderness. Our task is to open and to listen.

What follows is a guide for the journey.

Some of these offerings might speak to you deeply. Others will seem less relevant.

Pay attention to the stirrings of your own heart and the yearnings of your soul.

Take what is helpful and leave the rest.

May the Journey be for Blessing.

PASSOVER'S CALL to leave *mitzrayim*, the narrow place, is a call to leave the habits of mind and body that narrow our vision and distort our ability to act with love and generosity. *Yitziat mitzrayim*, the going forth out of Egypt, can be experienced as the continual practice of leaving attitudes, beliefs and behaviors that keep us bound in isolation and

fear. Working with the psalms, Jewish tradition teaches, is a tool to open the heart and liberate the spirit. The psalms, these ancient calls for help, these pleas for intimacy and awareness, these cries of pain and shouts of joy, reach into the depths and open the ways forward.

On each day of the *Omer*, a verse from Psalms is suggested for meditation. Feel encouraged to sit with the verse in the morning and keep returning to it during the day. Be curious as to how the psalm might speak to you.

Impatience, fear or anxiety may arise as you sit in meditation or may distract you in the busyness of your day. When this happens, you might want to shift your attention by saying the verse to yourself. Notice how it feels in your body.

The translations of the psalms within this guide come from my years of sitting and listening to these calls. Some translations are very close to the Hebrew; others drift much farther away. In each case, I sought to hear in the ancient words the longings of the heart — and to bring forth the verses in ways that could stir the soul and offer guidance on the journey.

— 4 —

COUNTING

THE MOST IMPORTANT THING is to count. Just a few moments of stopping and bringing your attention to each day is rich spiritual practice. Count even if you don't have the time or inclination to do so with *kavanah* (intention, reflection). Simply counting each night reminds us that everything passes. Simply counting strengthens our ability to stand in the moment, to give thanks and let go.

- We count at night because the Jewish day begins at sundown. It is traditional to wait until you see three stars in the sky before counting.

- We count standing to remember that our ancestors stood in the fields to wave their *Omer* offerings.

- If you forget to count one night and remember the next day, take a moment and count. If you forget a few nights in a row, locate where you are on the journey and begin anew.

- You might find it helpful to put a reminder about counting in a place where it will be easily noticed.

- You also might want to mark off the days and weeks on a calendar, perhaps even using different colored markers for each week.

- Many people have found it helpful to keep a journal through the 49 days. After each of the seven weeks within this book, two pages have been added for your personal reflections.

- Some have found it helpful to find partners for the counting, either to count together or simply to remind each other to count and to share their experiences.

- Above all, make the counting work for you. Be surprised at what arises.

HOW TO COUNT

- Find a place to stand where you won't be disturbed for a few moments.

- Take a soft, deep breath and begin with the introductory prayer.

- Say the blessing for counting, in Hebrew on page 8 and in English on page 9, then take another very conscious breath. Count the day (and week) of the *Omer* according to the instructions on page 9 of this Guide.

- Take a moment to name the spiritual quality of the day. With gentleness and discipline, commit yourself to notice how this quality will unfold within and around you as you go through the next 24 hours.

- Say the closing prayer.

- On some nights, you might find you do not have the time for the whole practice. In that case, say the prayer for counting and count the day.

- Practices are strengthened through repetition and routine. Counting in the same location and around the same time each evening can help sustain your practice.

WORKING WITH THE DAILY AND WEEKLY SPIRITUAL QUALITIES

Each of the seven weeks and each of the 49 days has its own spiritual quality. At the beginning of each week, there is an introductory page that provides intentions and suggestions for practices to help focus your attention. There is a page for each day, highlighting that day's unique combination of qualities along with a teaching and a prayer.

- Notice what each day brings. Notice your responses and insights to the qualities and how they feel in your body. Certain days or weeks might bring up difficult emotions. The practice is to be with them as best you can.

- You might want to make a note of days or weeks that are particularly difficult or joyful to see if you can discern a pattern that could be helpful to your self-understanding.

- Be gentle with yourself as you take this journey. It is a powerful practice that works on many layers of consciousness and awareness. The mystics teach that our counting brings forth blessing and healing for all the world.

Ken yihi ratzon. May it be so.

ספירת העומר

הנני מוכן ומזומן לקיים מצות עשה של ספירת
העומר כמו שכתוב בתורה:

וּסְפַרְתֶּם לָכֶם מִמָּחֳרַת הַשַּׁבָּת מִיּוֹם הֲבִיאֲכֶם אֶת־
עֹמֶר הַתְּנוּפָה: שֶׁבַע שַׁבָּתוֹת תְּמִימֹת תִּהְיֶינָה. עַד
מִמָּחֳרַת הַשַּׁבָּת הַשְּׁבִיעִת תִּסְפְּרוּ חֲמִשִּׁים יוֹם
וְהִקְרַבְתֶּם מִנְחָה חֲדָשָׁה לַיהוָה.

וִיהִי נֹעַם אֲדֹנָי אֱלֹהֵינוּ עָלֵינוּ: וּמַעֲשֵׂה יָדֵינוּ כּוֹנְנָה
עָלֵינוּ; וּמַעֲשֵׂה יָדֵינוּ כּוֹנְנֵהוּ.

ברוך אתא יהוה אלהינו מלך העולם אשר קדשנו
במצותיו וצונו על ספירת העומר:
היום ＿＿ לעומר. ספירת ＿＿ .

רבונו של עולם אתא צויתנו על ידי משה עבדך
לספּור ספירת העומר כדי לטהרנו מקלפותינו
ומטומואתינו כמו שכתבת בתורתך:

וּסְפַרְתֶּם לָכֶם מִמָּחֳרַת הַשַּׁבָּת מִיּוֹם הֲבִיאֲכֶם אֶת־
עֹמֶר הַתְּנוּפָה: שֶׁבַע שַׁבָּתוֹת תְּמִימֹת תִּהְיֶינָה. עַד
מִמָּחֳרַת הַשַּׁבָּת הַשְּׁבִיעִת תִּסְפְּרוּ חֲמִשִּׁים יוֹם
וְהִקְרַבְתֶּם מִנְחָה חֲדָשָׁה לַיהוָה.

כדי שיטהרו נפשות עמך ישראל מזוהמתם: ובכן
יהי רצון מלפניך יהוה אלהינו ואלהי אבותינו
שבזכות ספירת העומר שספתי היום יתוקן מה
שפגמתי בספירה (פלונית השייכת לאותו הלילה)
ואטהר ואתקדש בקדושה של מעלה ועל ידי זה
יושפע שפע רב בכל העולמות ילתקן את נפשותינו
ורוחותינו ונשמותינו מכל סיג יפגם ולטהרנו
ולקדשנו בקדושתך העליונה אמן סלה.

It is traditional to count at night while standing.

Opening Prayer

For the sake of the unification of the Holy One, with presence and awareness, in awe and love to unify the name יהוה — *yod-heh-vav-heh* — in complete unity, in the name of all of Israel, הִנֵּנִי — *Hineni* — Here I am — prepared and ready to perform the mitzvah of Counting the *Omer*. As is written in Torah: *You are to count from the morrow of the rest day from the day you brought the omer offering that is waved — there are to be seven complete weeks. You are to count until the day after the seventh week, 50 days, and then bring an offering, a new gift to God.*

— Leviticus 23:15-16

May the delight of God be upon us. May the work of our hands be supported. May the work of our hands bring forth God.

— Psalm 90:17

Prayer for Counting

Baruch ata yah eloheynu melekh haolam, asher kideshanu b'mitzvotav vetzivanu al sefirat ha'omer.

Blessed is the mystery that flows through time and space. You infuse us with holiness and call us into connection through the counting of the *Omer*.

Today is the _____ day of the *Omer*.
That makes _____ week(s) and _____ day(s) of the *Omer*.
Today has the spiritual quality of _____

Closing Prayer

Source of All, You called us to count the *Omer* in order to clear us of all that is in the way of our growth and service. Through my counting today, may there be cleared any debris that is in the way of the light shining through. May I be cleansed and sanctified with the holiness of above and through this may abundant bounty flow into the world. May *shefa* (abundant, radiant light) come through and heal our *nefesh*, *ruach* and *neshamah* (our layers of body, mind and soul) sanctifying us with the holiness of the *Elyon* (the Most High). Amen. *Selah.*

— 9 —

חסד

Generosity — Love — Compassion

Into the Expanse and Received in Love

THIS FIRST WEEK OF THE *OMER*, we notice what inspires our generosity and what causes us to close down and turn away.

We wonder at our capacity to give and receive love.

We cultivate the practice of responding to ourselves and others with compassion and kindness.

Today is the first day of the Omer.

Chesed Sh'b Chesed
LOVE WITHIN LOVE

The continual flow of love in the universe
Love without limit
    The journey begins with an invitation to know
        that we are loved absolutely.
This shall be my meditation day and night: *I am loved, I am cherished*
    for being exactly who I am. And through this love I bring forth blessing.

Practice for today:
Sit and bring attention to your breath.
Feel the breath moving through your body.
Notice the sensations as the breath enters in and as the breath goes forth.
After a few minutes say to yourself, *I am loved.* Watch what happens in
    your body as you continue to say with each breath, *I am loved.*
When you are ready, close the sit by saying to your heart,
    Through this love, I bring forth blessing.

אַשְׁרֵי תְמִימֵי־דֶרֶךְ הַהֹלְכִים בְּתוֹרַת יְהוָה

אַשְׁרֵי נֹצְרֵי עֵדֹתָיו בְּכָל־לֵב יִדְרְשׁוּהוּ

Fulfilled are those who walk in simplicity, guided by the Mystery.
Content are those who are mindful of what is important
And go forward with an open heart.

— Psalm 119:1-2

Gevurah Sh'b Chesed
DISCERNMENT WITHIN LOVE

Defining the path

Creating practices that guide us
   in giving and receiving the Divine love
      that flows through us and all the world

Practice for today:
Loving Kindness (Metta) Meditation
   We say this prayer for ourselves and others. Begin with yourself.
   Then pray — one at a time — for nine more people, making a
   minyan of blessing.
      May I (you) be blessed with love,
      May I (you) be blessed with peace,
      May I (you) be blessed with well being.

בְּכָל־לִבִּי דְרַשְׁתִּיךָ
With all my heart I seek the One.

— Psalm 119:10

Today is the third day of the Omer.

Tiferet Sh'b Chesed
BALANCE WITHIN LOVE

To love the world so much that every day
    something breaks open our hearts

Practice for today:
Make a commitment to pause three times today to notice
    and name something beautiful.
        It can be something you see, feel, hear, taste, touch.
Breathe the beauty into your body and let it rest upon your heart.

גְּמֹל עַל־עַבְדְּךָ אֶחְיֶה וְאֶשְׁמְרָה דְבָרֶךָ

גַּל־עֵינַי וְאַבִּיטָה נִפְלָאוֹת מִתּוֹרָתֶךָ

גֵּר אָנֹכִי בָאָרֶץ

I open to this service bestowed upon me:
    To live mindfully
    To open my eyes and behold the wonders
    To know that in every moment, I am only passing through.
                      — Psalm 119:17-19

Netzach Sh'b Chesed
ETERNITY WITHIN LOVE

The transformative power of love and generosity
The acts of kindness that change us and the world
Cultivating the commitment to let what we most love and value guide
   our actions.

Practice for today:
We ask ourselves:
>   When am I acting from fear?
>   When am I acting from anger?
>   What inspires me to act from love?

דֶּרֶךְ־מִצְוֹתֶיךָ אָרוּץ כִּי תַרְחִיב לִבִּי

I will travel the path of connection for You have expanded my heart.

— Psalm 119:32

— 15 —

Today is the fifth day of the Omer.

Hod Sh'b Chesed
PRESENCE WITHIN LOVE

Being where we are rather than where we think we should be
   or where we wish we could be

Cultivating the capacity to be patient with ourselves and others,
knowing that we are all doing the best we can in each moment

Practice for today:
Notice experiences and encounters that open your heart as well as
experiences and encounters that cause you to close down and turn
away. Practice noticing everything with non-judgmental awareness.
Practice noticing everything with gentleness and compassion.

וַאֲנִי בְּרֹב חַסְדְּךָ אָבוֹא בֵיתֶךָ
אֶשְׁתַּחֲוֶה אֶל־הֵיכַל־קָדְשְׁךָ בְּיִרְאָתֶךָ

*In your abundant chesed (love), I will enter your house. I will lay myself down
in awe.*

— Psalm 5:8

Today is the sixth day of the Omer.

Yesod Sh'b Cheded
ROOTEDNESS WITHIN LOVE

Sparks of Divinity are hidden within every person,
    within all experience, within all creation. Seeking these sparks,
    revealing these sparks, fills the world with love.

We breathe in the love that flows to us from past generations.
Rooted in this love we go forward into the expanse.

Practice for today:
Take time to remember and honor the gifts and blessings
you received from loved ones who have passed out of this world.
Say their names aloud and give thanks for their lives.

וִיבֹאֻנִי חֲסָדֶךָ יְהוָה תְּשׁוּעָתְךָ
May cheded, generous, abiding love, come through me.

— Psalm 119:41

Today is the seventh day, making one week of the Omer.

Shechina Sh'b Chesed
INDWELLING PRESENCE OF LOVE

מָגִנִּי עַל־אֱלֹהִים מוֹשִׁיעַ יִשְׁרֵי־לֵב

The Mystery is my shield. The Mystery opens the path of the heart.

— Psalm 7:11

Freeing the path of the heart
The Divine Presence calls, *Wherever you are, there I am.*
    I abide with you.

Practice for today:
Notice acts of kindness and generosity that are bestowed upon you.
Notice the moments you respond to yourself and others with love.

זְמִרוֹת הָיוּ־לִי חֻקֶּיךָ בְּבֵית מְגוּרָי
זָכַרְתִּי בַלַּיְלָה שִׁמְךָ יְהוָה
זֹאת הָיְתָה־לִּי כִּי פִקֻּדֶיךָ נָצָרְתִּי

In the place I dwell — Let there be music
In the darkness of night I will remember and guard the way.
How to live will arise in me
    as I remain mindful of the Divine presence within all being.

— Psalm 119:54-6

— 18 —

.

גבורה

Strength — Judgment — Discernment

Standing in Awe

Serving with Strength

Guided by Humility

Today is the eighth day, making one week and one day of the Omer.

Chesed Sh'b Gevurah
LOVE WITHIN STRENGTH

מָה־אֱנוֹשׁ כִּי־תִזְכְּרֶנּוּ וּבֶן־אָדָם כִּי תִפְקְדֶנּוּ
וַתְּחַסְּרֵהוּ מְּעַט מֵאֱלֹהִים וְכָבוֹד וְהָדָר תְּעַטְּרֵהוּ

What is it to be a human being — so vulnerable, so fragile, and at the same time only slightly less than gods, strong and powerful, crowned with splendor?

— Psalm 8:5-6

Feeling our power and strength and making the decision to infuse our actions with kindness and generosity

We ask ourselves in each encounter: What is the wise and compassionate choice?

Practice for today:
Judge everyone on the side of merit.

— *Pirke Avot* 1:6

Today is the ninth day, making one week and two days of the Omer.

Gevurah Sh'b Gevurah
STRENGTH WITHIN STRENGTH

רֵאשִׁית חָכְמָה | יִרְאַת יְהוָה

The beginning of wisdom is awe.

— Psalm 111:10

The strength of the spiritual warrior who remembers
   she is not the source of her power
She is the channel through which the Divine power flows.

Our lives are conceived in mystery,
Our strength comes from the Most High.
We bow to the Source of All
   as we yield to the power that flows through us.

Practice for today:
   Reflect on something you believe to be true.
   Feel the rightness,
      the truth of this idea, this thought.
   Then say to yourself: I could be wrong.
   Sit with the sensations that arise.

Today is the tenth day, making one week and three days of the Omer.

Tiferet Sh'b Gevurah
BALANCE WITHIN STRENGTH

The strength to yield
 The willingness to hold our judgments lightly
  The radiance of a generous heart that sees clearly
  and guides us in valuing what is difficult, what is different

Practice for today:
We ask ourselves,
 Where is the beauty in this… ?

שָׁמַעְתָּ יְהוָה תָּכִין לִבָּם
Listening deeply strengthens our hearts.

— Psalm 10:17

Today is the eleventh day, making one week and four days of the Omer.

Netzach Sh'b Gevurah
ENDURING STRENGTH

The strength to go forward
    The ability to see beyond ourselves,
        beyond our immediate circumstances
    Knowing that our actions unfold
        beyond anything we can ever see or know

Practice for today:
Perform an action aimed at bringing benefit to others.

גְּדֹלִים מַעֲשֵׂי יְהוָה דְּרוּשִׁים לְכָל־חֶפְצֵיהֶם

Great is the unfolding of the mystery, accessible to our deepest yearnings.
                              — Psalm 111:2

Today is the twelfth day, making one week and five days of the Omer.

Hod Sh'b Gevurah
GLORY WITHIN STRENGTH

Let this day be a holy vessel.
> Sit in whatever is.
> You are filled with Divine light. Feel yourself shine.

Practice for today:
Take some time to sit. Let your attention rest on your breath. Notice the breath moving through you.

After a few minutes, imagine the breath as a clear, pure light. The light might take on color or texture. Notice its qualities.

As your mind wanders, draw your attention back to your breath. With each breath in, feel yourself filled with light. With each breath out, watch the light spill out into the world. Notice that even as you breathe out, you remain filled with light.

Close the sit by giving thanks.

אַשְׁרֵי־אִישׁ יָרֵא אֶת־יְהוֶה בְּמִצְוֺתָיו חָפֵץ מְאֹד
זָרַח בַּחֹשֶׁךְ אוֹר לַיְשָׁרִים חַנּוּן וְרַחוּם וְצַדִּיק
Fulfilled is a person who lives in awe, who deeply desires connection.
> *For him, lights shine in darkness,*
>> *lights of grace, compassion and justice.*

— Psalm 112:1,4

Today is the thirteenth day, making one week and six days of the Omer.

Yesod Sh'b Gevurah
FOUNDATION WITHIN STRENGTH

Aligning ourselves with the highest will,
     Grounded in the sacred fire of the earth,
We pray to act for the good of all.

Practice for today:
Take time to feel your strengths, to give honor to your abilities.
Make a commitment to use your power
     to bring benefit and blessing.

צִוִּיתָ צֶדֶק עֵדֹתֶיךָ וֶאֱמוּנָה מְאֹד

We are called to act with righteousness, grounded in deep faith.

                                              — Psalm 119:138

Today is the fourteenth day, making two weeks of the Omer.

Shechina Sh'b Gevurah
MAJESTY WITHIN STRENGTH

We are all channels for the holy, here to be of service.
Our lives are our offerings.
May we serve with humility and strength.

Practice for today:
We ask ourselves,
> In what ways do I need to be more rigorous with myself?
> In what ways do I need to be more gentle?
>> What are the practices and rituals that guide and sustain me?

יְהֹוָה מִשָּׁמַיִם הִשְׁקִיף עַל־בְּנֵי־אָדָם
לִרְאוֹת הֲיֵשׁ מַשְׂכִּיל דֹּרֵשׁ אֶת־אֱלֹהִים

From the mystery, the Holy One gazes upon us
to see if there is someone who has the good sense to seek God in all.

— Psalm 14:2

— 28 —

תפארת

Radiance — Balance — Harmony — Truth

THE LIGHT OF *TIFERET* IS STRONG, demanding, radiant. Notice colors this week, the subtle and vibrant palates in nature. Notice your own being and the waves of emotions that move through you.

Tiferet shows us the beauty and brokenness of the world and says, *Open to all of it, this is where you live.*

— 31 —

Today is the fifteenth day, making two weeks and one day of the Omer.

Chesed Sh'b Tiferet
LOVE WITHIN BEAUTY

The heart breaks open with the pain and joy of being alive
    and the radiance shines through the cracks.
Being awake to our lives, we experience beauty and sorrow.
May we open to receive it all with gentleness, kindness and love.

Practice for today:
Let your attention rest on something beautiful.
    Breathe in its details, essence, fragrance.
    Feel the radiance spread through your body and give thanks.

הַשָּׁמַיִם שָׁמַיִם לַיהוָה וְהָאָרֶץ נָתַן לִבְנֵי־אָדָם
לֹא הַמֵּתִים יְהַלְלוּ־יָהּ וְלֹא כָּל־יֹרְדֵי דוּמָה
וַאֲנַחְנוּ ׀ נְבָרֵךְ יָהּ מֵעַתָּה וְעַד־עוֹלָם הַלְלוּ־יָהּ

The mystery belongs to the Eternal
But the earth was given to us.
Not recognizing the beauty deadens the spirit.
Turning away from gratitude hardens the heart.
Together we offer praise and give thanks for all that is.

— Psalm 115:16-18

Gevurah Sh'b Tiferet
DISCERNMENT WITHIN THE HEART

שִׁוִּיתִי יְהוָה לְנֶגְדִּי תָמִיד

I place the One before me always.

— Psalm 16:8

Cultivating the strength to live what is true even when it is difficult
We notice the joys, pain and challenges of our hearts,
    letting it all rise without judgment or shame.
The shining through of whatever is true brings healing.

Practice for today:
Take notice of what hardens your heart
    and what allows your heart to soften.
Say these verses for yourself and for people in your life with whom
    there is need for healing:

לָכֵן ׀ שָׂמַח לִבִּי וַיָּגֶל כְּבוֹדִי אַף־בְּשָׂרִי יִשְׁכֹּן לָבֶטַח

May my (your) heart know happiness.
May my (your) soul know joy.
And may my (your) whole being dwell in trust.

— Psalm 16:9

Tiferet Sh'b Tiferet
BALANCE WITHIN THE HEART

אֲנִי בְּצֶדֶק אֶחֱזֶה פָנֶיךָ אֶשְׂבְּעָה בְהָקִיץ תְּמוּנָתֶךָ

Through right action I will awaken to the Divine Presence in all being.

— Psalm 17:15

The natural inclination of the heart is to seek balance and truth,
to be in harmony, to delight in beauty. And it is so easy to go astray,
to lose our balance as confusion clouds our perceptions.
It takes practice to return again and again to beauty and love.

Practice for today:
Take special notice of color and light.
Let yourself be surprised by patterns, images and designs.
    When you feel off balance or notice that confusion arises,
    shift your attention by seeing and naming something beautiful,
    something that inspires love.

הִנְנִי עֹשֶׂה חֲדָשָׁה עַתָּה תִצְמָח הֲלוֹא תֵדָעוּהָ

Take notice,
        the Mystery calls, I am doing a new thing.
        Right now it is sprouting.
            Suddenly you will know it.

— Isaiah 43:19

Netzach Sh'b Tiferet
ENDURANCE WITHIN THE HEART

וַיּוֹצִיאֵנִי לַמֶּרְחָב יְחַלְּצֵנִי כִּי חָפֵץ בִּי

God brings me out into the expanse,
God releases me because God desires me.

— Psalm 18:20

We are God's desire.
We are being called forth to live fully,
To stand in strength,
    to let our lights shine.

Practice for today:
We ask ourselves,
What do I have to let go of to move forward?

אֶרְחָמְךָ יְהֹוָה חִזְקִי

I will act compassionately toward all.
I will remember that my strength comes from the Eternal.

— Psalm 18:2

Today is the nineteenth day, making two weeks and five days of the Omer.

Hod Sh'b Tiferet
BEING WITHIN BEAUTY

The light, the wisdom, the glory
   that rises from the unfolding of creation

הַשָּׁמַיִם מְסַפְּרִים כְּבוֹד־אֵל וּמַעֲשֵׂה יָדָיו מַגִּיד הָרָקִיעַ
יוֹם לְיוֹם יַבִּיעַ אֹמֶר וְלַיְלָה לְּלַיְלָה יְחַוֶּה־דָּעַת
אֵין־אֹמֶר וְאֵין דְּבָרִים בְּלִי נִשְׁמָע קוֹלָם

The heavens declare the glory of God.
The firmament tells of God's works.
Day after day utters speech,
Night after night declares knowledge.

There is no speech.
There are no words.
Not a sound is heard.   — Psalm 19:2-4

Practice for today:
Take notice of the sky and the glorious luminance of the day.
Listen to the silence.
Forgive yourself, forgive others.
Remember that everything changes and unfolds in its own time.

יִהְיוּ לְרָצוֹן ׀ אִמְרֵי־פִי וְהֶגְיוֹן לִבִּי לְפָנֶיךָ יְהוָֹה צוּרִי וְגֹאֲלִי
May the words of my mouth and the meditations of my heart
be aligned with the Highest Will.

                                              — Psalm 19:15

Yesod Sh'b Tiferet
CONNECTION WITHIN THE HEART

יְהֹוָה הוֹשִׁיעָה הַמֶּלֶךְ יַעֲנֵנוּ בְיוֹם־קָרְאֵנוּ

The Mystery brings transformation.
The One answers us in the moment we call.

— Psalm 20:10

The wellspring rises from deep within the Mystery, filling the heart
with truths. Sometimes these truths are welcome and easy to contain,
sometimes they are painful and cause a shattering.
There is great strength to be found in opening to whatever is coming
forth.

Practice for today:
We ask ourselves:
> What am I meant to learn, to discover?
> What truths do I need to integrate?
We pray for ourselves and nine others:

יִזְכֹּר כָּל־מִנְחֹתֶךָ וְעוֹלָתְךָ יְדַשְּׁנֶה סֶלָה
יִתֶּן־לְךָ כִלְבָבֶךָ וְכָל־עֲצָתְךָ יְמַלֵּא

May my (our) gifts be remembered.
May my (our) offerings be received.
May my (our) heart's yearning be granted.
May my (our) clearest intentions be fulfilled.

— Psalm 20:4-5

Shechina Sh'b Tiferet
MAJESTY WITHIN BEAUTY

Beauty and love are made manifest through our words and actions.
Each of us, all creation, celebrates the Divine.
Our lives are our offerings.
May we be grounded in compassion and truth.

Practice for today:
Make an extra effort to care for your physical well-being.
    Eat well. Walk. Exercise. Stretch.
Stop for a moment, take a slow even deep breath
    and notice the life force that flows through you and into the world.

כִּי־הַמֶּלֶךְ בֹּטֵחַ בַּיהוָה וּבְחֶסֶד עֶלְיוֹן בַּל־יִמּוֹט

*The heart trusts the flow of the Mystery
and the love of the Most High.
It will not be shaken.*

— Psalm 21:8

נצח

Eternity — Vision — Endurance

Eternity in Each Moment
Connection to
All that Was, All that Is, All that Will Be

THIS WEEK CALLS US to feel ourselves capable of transformation, to believe that everything we do matters and that our actions today affect generations to come. Envision the person you long to be, envision the world you long to live in and walk toward these visions with all your strength.

Today is the twenty-second day, making three weeks and one day of the Omer.

Chesed Sh'b Netzach
LOVE WITHIN VISION

יְחִי לְבַבְכֶם לָעַד
Your hearts will live forever.

— Psalm 22:27

Our acts of kindness and generosity endure.
Trust in your capacity to act with compassion and notice how it feels in
your body when you respond to yourself and others with empathy.
Our loving actions bring forth healing.

Practice for today:
Ask yourself: Am I speaking truthfully?
    Is what I am saying helpful?
    Is what I am saying kind?
    Is what I am saying necessary and appropriate to the moment?

לְמַעַן אַחַי וְרֵעָי אֲדַבְּרָה־נָּא שָׁלוֹם בָּךְ
לְמַעַן בֵּית־יְהֹוָה אֱלֹהֵינוּ אֲבַקְשָׁה טוֹב לָךְ
For the sake of my brothers, my sisters and friends,
I will speak for peace;
For the sake of creation,
I will seek well-being for all.

— Psalm 122:8-9

Gevurah Sh'b Netzach
STRENGTH WITHIN ENDURANCE

כּוֹסִי רְוָיָה
My cup overflows.

— Psalm 23:5

We ask for the strength to do what is right,
the discipline to follow through on our commitments,
the perseverance to act for good,
even when we don't see the results we long for.

Practice for today:
Do one action that brings you into connection with others,
that turns you toward the Mystery,
that encourages awe and love,
that is aimed at bringing forth good.

אַךְ ׀ טוֹב וָחֶסֶד יִרְדְּפוּנִי כָּל־יְמֵי חַיָּי וְשַׁבְתִּי
בְּבֵית־יְהוָה לְאֹרֶךְ יָמִים
May goodness and kindness pursue me all the days of my life.
I will dwell in the heart of the Mystery always.

— Psalm 23:6

— 43 —

Today is the twenty-fourth day, making three weeks and three days of the Omer.

Tiferet Sh'b Netzach
BEAUTY THAT ENDURES

לַיהוָה הָאָרֶץ וּמְלוֹאָהּ תֵּבֵל וְיֹשְׁבֵי בָהּ

The earth and all that is, is filled with Divine presence.

— Psalm 24:1

Beauty abounds. At times we can feel ourselves filled and surrounded
by splendor. Other times all we can see is brokenness and pain.
It is our responsibility to search out, notice and create beauty.
And it is our responsibility to allow the beauty to inspire our empathy
and encourage our acts of connection and love.

Practice for today:
Notice the beauty of nature and the beauty created by human hands.
Notice what it feels like in your body to be with something beautiful.
Name for yourself a way you bring beauty into this world.

מִי־יַעֲלֶה בְהַר־יְהוָה וּמִי־יָקוּם בִּמְקוֹם קָדְשׁוֹ

נְקִי כַפַּיִם וּבַר־לֵבָב

זֶה דּוֹר דֹּרְשָׁו מְבַקְשֵׁי פָנֶיךָ

Who ascends the high places?
Who stands in holiness?
Those with open hands and pure hearts,
all who seek the presence.

— Psalm 24:3-4,6

Netzach Sh'b Netzach
ETERNITY WITHIN ETERNITY

דְּרָכֶיךָ יְהוָה הוֹדִיעֵנִי אֹרְחוֹתֶיךָ לַמְּדֵנִי
הַדְרִיכֵנִי בַאֲמִתֶּךָ
זְכֹר־רַחֲמֶיךָ יְהוָה וַחֲסָדֶיךָ כִּי מֵעוֹלָם הֵמָּה

May we be shown the paths to travel,
May we be guided in truth.
May we bring to awareness compassion and love
Remembering they are forever.

> — Psalm 25:4-6

Everything is alive, filled with potential.
All creation makes manifest the One.
The Eternal fills each moment and calls us forward to shine.

Practice for today:
At some time during this day, pause and stand.
Bring your attention to your feet,
   and feel them grounded to the earth.
Extend your shoulders back so your heart space opens;
   let your hands rest facing outward by your side.
Bring your attention to the crown of your head,
   take a deep breath, breathing in the Mystery.
Return your attention to the souls of your feet,
   and breathe in the power of the earth.
In the palms of your hands, feel the sensations of life around you.
With a breath into your heart, feel the Mystery moving through.
When you are ready, declare:

אֵלֶיךָ יְהוָה נַפְשִׁי אֶשָּׂא

To You, Eternal Presence, I lift my soul.

> — Psalm 25:1

— 45 —

Hod Sh'b Netzach
GRATITUDE WITHIN ETERNITY

We open to whatever is unfolding in our lives and reach for gratitude.
Gratitude helps lift us beyond our own pain, fears and doubt.
Gratitude helps us find the strength to stand in the moment
and discern the path forward.

Practice for today:
Give thanks before you eat.
Say thank you when you see something beautiful,
when you experience a moment of connection.
Give thanks for all this day brings
and notice how gratitude feels in your body.

כִּי־חַסְדְּךָ לְנֶגֶד עֵינָי וְהִתְהַלַּכְתִּי בַּאֲמִתֶּךָ
לַשְׁמִעַ בְּקוֹל תּוֹדָה וּלְסַפֵּר כָּל־נִפְלְאוֹתֶיךָ

I will see the world through eyes of love and generosity,
and walk in the truths they reveal.
I will give voice to my gratitude, and speak about the wonders I behold.
— Psalm 26:3,7

Today is the twenty-seventh day, making three weeks and six days of the Omer.

Yesod Sh'b Netzach
FOUNDATION WITHIN ETERNITY

Wisdom flows through all creation.
It is revealed through the trees, the mountains,
    the songs of the river and the sea.
Each blade of grass, each rock and flower, has something to teach.
    The Mystery is waiting to be received.

Practice for today:
Notice what in the natural world attracts your attention.
Spend a few moments wondering what wisdom it conveys.

לְךָ ׀ אָמַר לִבִּי בַּקְּשׁוּ פָנָי אֶת־פָּנֶיךָ יְהוָה אֲבַקֵּשׁ
קַוֵּה אֶל־יְהוָה חֲזַק וְיַאֲמֵץ לִבֶּךָ וְקַוֵּה אֶל־יְהוָה

The Mystery says to my heart: Seek my presence.
The presence of all that was, all that is, all that will be, I will seek.
    I am grounded in the Mystery.
    May my heart be strong and filled with courage.
    I am grounded in the Mystery.

— Psalm 27:8,14

Today is the twenty-eighth day, making four weeks of the Omer.

Shechina Sh'b Netzach
THE FLOW OF ETERNITY

אַשְׁרֵי כָּל־יְרֵא יְהֹוָה הַהֹלֵךְ בִּדְרָכָיו

A song of arising:
Filled with abundance are those who honor the Mystery
and follow the ways of the spirit.

— Psalm 128:1

We stand in the moment and feel our connection to all that came
before us and all that will come after. We remember our grandparents,
our great grandparents and all those whose actions have helped to
create our lives. And we remind ourselves that we, right now, are
shaping the world for those who will some day call us ancestors.

Practice for today:
Reflect on the world in which your grand-parents lived.
Imagine the world you would like to bestow on the next generation.

יְהֹוָה ׀ עֻזִּי וּמָגִנִּי בּוֹ בָטַח לִבִּי

The Mystery is my strength and my shield.
My heart trusts all that will unfold.

— Psalm 28:7

הוד

Presence — Gratitude

Being in the Presence
Being in the Present
and Giving Thanks

Opening to the glory of each moment,
whatever the moment brings

Today is the twenty-ninth day, making four weeks and one day of the Omer.

Chesed Sh'b Hod
LOVE WITHIN PRESENCE

Whatever is growing, whatever is coming through,
    practice meeting it with love.
Where there is pain, offer compassion.
Where there is fear, reach out with tenderness.
When there is resistance, respond with patience.

Practice for today:
Make a commitment to sit for 5-10 minutes.

Begin by anchoring your attention on your breath.
As thoughts, emotions, sensations arise, say to each, בִּרְכַּת־יה אֲלֵיכֶם —
The blessing of the Mystery upon you (Psalm 129:8) — and return your
attention to your breath. Each time your mind wanders, bless the
wandering with this verse and bring yourself back to center
by taking another deep breath.

יְהוָֹה עֹז לְעַמּוֹ יִתֵּן יְהוָֹה ׀ יְבָרֵךְ אֶת־עַמּוֹ בַשָּׁלוֹם
From the Mystery flows strength, from the Mystery flows peace.

                                    —Psalm 29:11

Today is the thirtieth day, making four weeks and two days of the Omer.

Gevurah Sh'b Hod
STRENGTH WITHIN PRESENCE

The strength and humility
    to meet whatever life brings with *kavod* (honor)
Practices and disciplines support our efforts and help guide our way.

Practice for today:
Sit for 5-10 minutes.

Notice the sensations of the breath moving in and out of your body.
Feel the breath fill your chest, stomach, neck and head.

Watch the breath move down your arms and legs. After a few minutes
of noticing these sensations, speak these words to your heart: חַיִּים בִּרְצוֹנוֹ
— *Life flows from the Highest Will* (Psalm 30:6) — and continue to repeat
these words with each breath. When you notice your mind has
wandered, call your attention back by taking a deep breath into these
words: *Life flows from the Highest Will.*

דֶּרֶךְ־אֱמוּנָה בָחָרְתִּי מִשְׁפָּטֶיךָ שִׁוִּיתִי
I choose the path of faith and place my practices before me to guide the way.
                                                    — Psalm 119:30

— 53 —

Today is the thirty-first day, making four weeks and three days of the Omer.

Tiferet Sh'b Hod
BEAUTY WITHIN PRESENCE

Opening to wonder, beauty, love and splendor
    in the midst of our broken world
Anchoring ourselves in beauty can help us
    meet pain and suffering with love.

חִזְקוּ וְיַאֲמֵץ לְבַבְכֶם כָּל־הַמְיַחֲלִים לַיהוָה

May our hearts be strong and filled with courage.
May we open to guidance and love.

— Psalm 31:25

Practice for today:

Sit and draw your attention to something beautiful: leaves on a tree;
a candle flame; a piece of art; a photo of someone you love.

Breathe the beauty into your body, and say to your heart,

שִׁוִּיתִי | וְדוֹמַמְתִּי נַפְשִׁי

May my soul be calm, may my soul be content. (Psalm 131:2)

Sit for a few minutes repeating this verse, feeling the sensations of
beauty in your body. If your eyes have been open, close them
and let your attention shift to a place in this world where there is great
pain and despair. Let yourself become aware of the suffering. Breathe
forth your prayers by saying, הָאִירָה פָנֶיךָ עַל־עַבְדֶּךָ הוֹשִׁיעֵנִי בְחַסְדֶּךָ —
May the light of the One shine on you for deliverance and love. (Psalm 31:17)

Close your sit by returning to an image of beauty and saying,
    May my soul be calm, may my soul be content.
    May all souls be calm, may all souls be content.

Today is the thirty-second day, making four weeks and four days of the Omer.

Netzach Sh'b Hod
ENDURANCE WITHIN PRESENCE

אַשְׂכִּילְךָ ׀ וְאוֹרְךָ בְּדֶרֶךְ־זוּ תֵלֵךְ

The Mystery calls:
I will give you the good sense,
I will fill you with light so you can discern the best path to travel.

— Psalm 32:8

Listening for the wisdom, knowledge and awareness
    that helps us know when it is time to be still
    and when it is time to step forward
Watching for the signs that show us how to respond effectively
    to whatever the moment calls for

Practice for today:
Find a comfortable place to sit. Close your eyes. Let your hands rest
on your legs, palms facing up. Take a few calming deep breaths and
bring your attention to your hands. Feel the sensations in your open
palms and on your fingers. When you notice your mind has wandered,
bring your attention gently back by taking a breath
and returning to the feelings in your hands and finger tips.

Sit with these sensations for 5-10 minutes.

End your sit by lifting your hands and offering thanks.

הַבּוֹטֵחַ בַּיהוָה חֶסֶד יְסוֹבְבֶנּוּ

Trust surrounds us with love.

— Psalm 32:10

LAG BA'OMER
Today is the thirty-third day, making four weeks and five days of the Omer.

Hod Sh'b Hod
PRESENCE WITHIN PRESENCE

A resting place
A moment to pause
A day to stop and notice where we are on our journey
We take a deep breath and give thanks for everything
    that has brought us to this moment.

Practice for today:

Find a comfortable place to sit. Notice the sensations as you take
a few deep and even breaths. Offer thanks. Notice the sights, sounds,
smells that surround you. Offer thanks.

Close your eyes and let yourself sit for 5, 10, 15 minutes, anchoring
your attention on your breath. When you notice that your mind has
wandered, say "thank you" and bring your attention back to your breath.

As you end your sit you can say to your heart — *Abundant love fills the
earth. May kindness, love and generosity be upon us all.* (Psalm 33:5,22)

כִּי־יָשָׁר דְּבַר־יְהוָה וְכָל־מַעֲשֵׂהוּ בֶּאֱמוּנָה
The way forward is clear and everything unfolds in faith.

— Psalm 33:4

Today is the thirty-fourth day, making four weeks and six days of the Omer.

Yesod Sh'b Hod

FOUNDATION WITHIN PRESENCE

הֲבִינֵנִי וְאֶצְּרָה תוֹרָתֶךָ וְאֶשְׁמְרֶנָּה בְכָל־לֵב

*May I have the understanding to cherish the journey
and care for it with all my heart.*

— Psalm 119:34

Our souls yearn to live in alignment
    with all creation, and at times we get so lost and far away.
    The earth, trees, water and sky call,
    offering to guide us back to center,
       back to presence and awareness.
May we open to their wisdom and their truths.

Practice for today:
Sit and allow your imagination to be drawn to something
in the natural world that fills you with appreciation and awe: a tree;
an open field; the swells of the ocean; a rock, the sky at dawn. Imagine
it as fully as you can and let yourself be filled
with the sensations of this vision.

Breathe into this gift of the natural world, feel its power and wisdom.

As you notice your mind wander, use your breath to return again and
again to the strength and insight that flows to you from creation.

טַעֲמוּ וּרְאוּ כִּי־טוֹב יְהוָה אַשְׁרֵי הַגֶּבֶר יֶחֱסֶה־בּוֹ

*Experience fully the goodness that unfolds.
Content is the person who takes refuge in the mystery.*

— Psalm 34:9

— 57 —

Today is the thirty-fifth day, making five weeks of the Omer.

Shechina Sh'b Hoд
FLOW OF GRATITUDE

The earth is filled with glory.
Our lives are filled with goodness.
As we notice the blessings and give thanks,
    we create a dwelling place for the Most High.

Practice for today:
Let these be the first words you say upon awakening:
    Modah ani—I am grateful.

Throughout the day, pause ten times and offer gratitude.
    Give thanks for the food you eat, for a beautiful sight or sound.
    Offer praise for an insight, a moment of connection, a moment of love.

End the day by saying, "I am grateful for...."

הַלְלוּ יָהּ l הַלְלוּ אֶת־שֵׁם יְהוָה הַלְלוּ עַבְדֵי יְהוָה
שֶׁעֹמְדִים בְּבֵית יְהוָה בְּחַצְרוֹת בֵּית אֱלֹהֵינוּ
הַלְלוּ־יָהּ כִּי־טוֹב יְהוָה זַמְּרוּ לִשְׁמוֹ כִּי נָעִים

Offer praise for all that is.
    Stand in service and offer praise.
    Be in each moment and offer praise.
Let your soul sing, feel all the goodness and offer praise.

— Psalm 135: 1-3

יְסוֹד

Foundation — Connection

The wellspring rising from deep within the Mystery
The rock that supports, sustains
and brings forth our lives

YESOD CALLS us to feel ourselves grounded in the Mystery
and to feel the Mystery rising within us. *Yesod* calls us to
encounter the fire, the sacred sparks at the core of creation.
We honor all that guides and sustains us.

And we ask ourselves: How can I bring my truest self
into the world for good?

Today is the thirty-sixth day, making five weeks and one day of the Omer.

Chesed Sh'b Yesod
LOVE WITHIN FOUNDATION

כִּי־עִמְּךָ מְקוֹר חַיִּים בְּאוֹרְךָ נִרְאֶה־אוֹר

For with you is the source of life. In your light, we see light.

— Psalm 36:10

Connecting to the love and generosity that flows to us from the Mystery.
Opening ourselves to the Source
    so our actions are filled with kindness and grace

Practice for today:
Make a commitment today to listen well.
    When someone is speaking, listen with your whole body.
    Listen without trying to form a response.
    Listen to the words being spoken
        and listen to the currents underneath the words.
Practice listening with compassion.

מַה־יָּקָר חַסְדְּךָ אֱלֹהִים וּבְנֵי אָדָם בְּצֵל כְּנָפֶיךָ יֶחֱסָיוּן

How essential is the flow of Divine Love.
Here we take refuge.

— Psalm 36:8

Today is the thirty-seventh day, making five weeks and two days of the Omer.

Gevurah Sh'b Yesod
STRENGTH WITHIN CONNECTION

בְּטַח בַּיהוָה וַעֲשֵׂה־טוֹב שְׁכָן־אֶרֶץ וּרְעֵה אֱמוּנָה

Trust the unfolding and act well.
Dwell in the land, and be nourished by faith

— Psalm 37:3

The strength of the spiritual warrior
who can discern her path and give honor to all
Today we honor:
    The courage that is shaped by practice
    The guidance that is revealed through faith
    The clarity that comes from surrender
    The insight that rises with action.

Practice for today:
Take 5-10 minutes to sit. Anchor attention on the breath and feel it fill
your body. After a few moments, say to your heart, *I trust the unfolding
and I will meet it well.* Continue to say this phrase, calling your attention
back as it wanders, noticing how this affirmation feels in your body
and noticing the emotions it stirs.

End your sit with three deep calming breaths.

גּוֹל עַל־יְהוָה דַּרְכֶּךָ וּבְטַח עָלָיו וְהוּא יַעֲשֶׂה

Commit yourself to the unfolding path,
Trust
And guidance will come.

— Psalm 37:5

Today is the thirty-eighth day, making five weeks and three days of the Omer.

Tiferet Sh'b Yesod
BEAUTY WITHIN CONNECTION

Touching the depths
   and aligning ourselves with the truth of each moment
Feeling the soul shift as it moves toward balance
Taking notice of the beauty in the simple and the ordinary,
   and declaring all life sacred

Practice for today:
Find a place to sit that to you is beautiful, that to you is sacred.
   Look around. Take in the details, the sights, sounds, smells.
Close your eyes and feel the sacred within you.
With a deep breath, give thanks.

Close your sit by saying a prayer for the safety and well-being of others.

אוֹדְךָ בְּכָל־לִבִּי
אֶשְׁתַּחֲוֶה אֶל־הֵיכַל קָדְשְׁךָ וְאוֹדֶה אֶת־שְׁמֶךָ
עַל־חַסְדְּךָ וְעַל־אֲמִתֶּךָ

I give thanks with all my heart.
I lay myself down in the Holy Temple and give thanks for all.
For love, for truth.

— Psalm 138:1-2

Netzach Sh'b Yesod
ETERNITY WITHIN CONNECTION

The continual unfolding of all of life
Everything that has ever happened has created this very moment.
Everything that will ever be unfolds from here.

We call on the Source of Life to guide us
And to open the path forward with grace.

Practice for today:
We ask ourselves:
  How do I respond to change?
  What gives me the faith and the courage to create connection?
  What gives me the faith and the courage to let go?

גֵּר אָנֹכִי עִמָּךְ ׀ תּוֹשָׁב כְּכָל־אֲבוֹתָי

I am a sojourner here within the Mystery.
Like all my ancestors who came before me, I seek a place to dwell.

— Psalm 39:13

Today is the fortieth day, making five weeks and five days of the Omer.

Hod Sh'b Yesod
PRESENCE WITHIN CONNECTION

Grounding ourselves in the moment through gratitude and awareness
Opening to the calls of our lives

Practice for today:
Sit for 5, 10, 15 minutes. Bring your attention to your breath.
After a few moments, say to your heart, *Hineni* — Here I am,
present, open, willing. Continue repeating *Hineni* with each breath.

When you become aware of your mind wandering, gently, and with
compassion, bring yourself back to the moment by saying to yourself,
Hineni — Here I am. Close your sit by giving thanks.

Bring this practice into the day – pausing at various times to say to
yourself, *Hineni* — Here I am.

זֶבַח וּמִנְחָה ׀ לֹא־חָפַצְתָּ

אָז אָמַרְתִּי הִנֵּה־בָאתִי בִּמְגִלַּת־סֵפֶר כָּתוּב עָלָי

לַעֲשׂוֹת־רְצוֹנְךָ אֱלֹהַי חָפָצְתִּי וְתוֹרָתְךָ בְּתוֹךְ מֵעָי

*Source of All, You have opened my understanding. You have made it known
that You do not desire sacrifices, sin offerings or burnt offerings.
Rather, what you desire is for me to say:*

> *Here I am, I have come with the scroll of the book
> that is written upon me. My deepest yearnings
> are to act in alignment with your will
> and to live the truths that you placed within me.*

— Psalm 40:7-9

Today is the forty-first day, making five weeks and six days of the Omer.

Yesod Sh'b Yesod
FOUNDATION WITHIN FOUNDATION

וַאֲנִי בְּתֻמִּי תָּמַכְתָּ בִּי וַתַּצִּיבֵנִי לְפָנֶיךָ לְעוֹלָם

בָּרוּךְ יְהֹוָה ׀ אֱלֹהֵי יִשְׂרָאֵל מֵהָעוֹלָם וְעַד הָעוֹלָם אָמֵן ׀ וְאָמֵן

In integrity, I am supported.
In alignment, I stand before all that is hidden.
Blessed are the secrets of eternity.

— Psalm 41:13-14

Here we stand, with reverence and awe
Our roots firmly planted within the Mystery.

Practice for today:
Take time to be aware of the earth on which you walk.
Feel the ground under your feet.
Make contact with someone you haven't spoken with for a while.
Offer a prayer for the healing and well-being of the natural world.

תִּכּוֹן תְּפִלָּתִי קְטֹרֶת לְפָנֶיךָ מַשְׂאַת כַּפַּי מִנְחַת־עָרֶב

May my prayers be rooted
May they rise like incense
May the offerings of my hands be received as a gift.

— Psalm 141:2

— 67 —

Today is the forty-second day, making six weeks of the Omer.

Shechina Sh'b Yesod
SOURCE WITHIN FOUNDATION

כְּאַיָּל תַּעֲרֹג עַל־אֲפִיקֵי־מָיִם כֵּן נַפְשִׁי תַעֲרֹג אֵלֶיךָ אֱלֹהִים
צָמְאָה נַפְשִׁי ׀ לֵאלֹהִים לְאֵל חָי

Like a deer yearns for brooks and streams,
    my soul yearns for the Mystery.
    My soul thirsts for the Source of All,
    for the Source of all Life.

— Psalm 42: 2-3

The seeds of creativity, the sparks of clarity
Vision, insight and wisdom arising
We give thanks for all we have learned
And pray to bring the blessings forward.

Practice for today:
Take time to reflect on the experiences that have shaped you,
    the people that support you and the values that you stand on.
We ask ourselves:
    What are my sacred values? Where are my roots planted?
    Who are my teachers? What wisdom do I hope to pass on?

Offer this prayer for yourself and places in the world that need healing:
    Sim shalom, tova, uvracha, chayim, chen, v'chesed, v'rachamim aleynu
    Place upon us peace, well-being, blessing, life,
    grace, love and compassion.

— Amida

שכינה   מלכות

Majesty — Divine Presence

The Channel, The Flow Of The Most High
The Indwelling Of Divine Presence

THIS FINAL WEEK is a time of integration. We are called to open our hands and our hearts and wonder about the gifts we can bring into the world.

We ask ourselves: How can I best be of service?

Today is the forty-third day, making six weeks and one day of the Omer.

Chesed Sh'b Malchut
LOVE WITHIN DIVINE PRESENCE

Love that flows through us into the world
Today we let our thoughts dwell on the experiences of the heart.

Practice for today:
We ask ourselves:
    In what situations do I feel generous and loving?
    When do I feel myself closing down and turning away?
    Who has loved me well? To whom have I opened my heart?

שְׁלַח־אוֹרְךָ וַאֲמִתְּךָ הֵמָּה יַנְחוּנִי יְבִיאוּנִי
אֶל־הַר־קָדְשְׁךָ וְאֶל־מִשְׁכְּנוֹתֶיךָ
וְאָבוֹאָה ׀ אֶל־מִזְבַּח אֱלֹהִים אֶל־אֵל שִׂמְחַת גִּילִי וְאוֹדְךָ

Send forth Divine light and truth, they will guide me
    and bring me to the holy mountain, to where the Sacred Presence dwells.
There I will come toward the Mystery in gladness and joy
    and give thanks.

— Psalm 43:3-4

The Mystery is revealed through love.

Today is the forty-fourth day, making six weeks and two days of the Omer.

Gevurah Sh'b Shechina
DISCERNMENT WITHIN SACRED DWELLING

כִּי־הוּא יֹדֵעַ תַּעֲלֻמוֹת לֵב

God knows the hidden places of the heart.

— Psalm 44:22

The strength, the power that comes through us into the world
We observe our will — the ways it focuses our attention and makes
　　possible our journeys

　　and the ways in which our will hinders us, blocks our vision,
　　　　encourages our arrogance, anger and fears.

Practice for today:
Notice your impatience, your defiance and inclination to do battle.
Notice moments of responding to yourself and others harshly.
Do your best to breathe into these moments with love.
Do your best to surround these inclinations with compassion.
We bow to the goodness that we are as we open to the guidance that
flows through us from the Highest Will.

The Mystery is revealed through strength and humility

Tiferet Sh'b Malchut
BEAUTY WITHIN MAJESTY

Everything is a gift from the Divine. Everything that is,
    everything that will be. It is all a gift from the Eternal.
Keeping our hearts closed profanes the gift.
Keeping our hearts closed deadens the spirit.

Practice for today:
We ask ourselves:
What gifts have I received?
    What gifts have I turned away from?
        Where do I find meaning?

רָחַשׁ לִבִּי ׀ דָּבָר טוֹב
My heart is astir with a good thing.

— Psalm 45:2

וַאֲבָרְכָה ׳ שִׁמְךָ לְעוֹלָם וָעֶד
And always I will bless all that is.

— Psalm 145:1

The Mystery is revealed through a willing heart.

Today is the forty-sixth day, making six weeks and four days of the Omer.

Netzach Sh'b Shechina
ETERNITY WITHIN DIVINE PRESENCE

Each moment is a seed of eternity
  and all there is, is now.
With everything we do, we weave the future
  and all there is, is now.
Our lives extend beyond anything we will ever know
  and all there is, is now.
In every moment we dwell in the Sacred Presence.
May we act accordingly.

Practice for today:
We lay these questions on our hearts:
What are the treasures of my life?
How do I live my gratitude and blessings?

אֱלֹהִים לָנוּ מַחֲסֶה וָעֹז עֶזְרָה בְצָרוֹת נִמְצָא מְאֹד
הַרְפּוּ וּדְעוּ כִּי־אָנֹכִי אֱלֹהִים
יְהוָה צְבָאוֹת עִמָּנוּ

The Infinite calls: "I am very close.
Be still and know that I am."
The source of Infinite possibility is with us. This is our refuge and strength.
— Psalm 46:2,11,12

The Mystery is revealed through action.

Today is the forty-seventh day, making six weeks and five days of the Omer.

Hod Sh'b Shechina
OPENNESS WITHIN DIVINE PRESENCE

It all comes from the Mystery. It all returns to the Mystery.
    It all is the Mystery.
We sit in each moment and call forth Divine light to guide us,
    to show us the way.

Practice for today:
Sit with all the sensations in your body,
    your breath, your heartbeat,
    the sensations in your arms, legs and torso.
With gentleness and compassion, ask yourself to open
    to the guides who are here for you
        and to receive everything you need.

הָרֹפֵא לִשְׁבוּרֵי לֵב
The Infinite heals our broken hearts.

— Psalm 147:3

The Mystery is revealed through patience.

Yesod Sh'b Malchut

FOUNDATION WITHIN MAJESTY

We give thanks for our teachers and guides.
We give thanks for all we have learned.
We give thanks for what our lives have revealed.

Practice for today:
We ask ourselves:
    What can I bring forth from the experiences of my life?
    What do I have to teach?
    How can my words and actions reflect
        what I hold as most sacred?

וְאֶשָּׂא־כַפַּי אֶל־מִצְוֹתֶיךָ אֲשֶׁר אָהָבְתִּי

I lift my hands to do mitzvot, I lift my hands to love.

— Psalm 119:48

The Mystery is revealed through connection.

Today is the forty-ninth day, making seven weeks of the Omer.

Shechina Sh'b Malchut
DIVINE PRESENCE WITHIN MAJESTY

All of us are sacred vessels,
    channels through which the Divine flows into this world.
Each of us is uniquely formed
    so as to bring forth a particular aspect of the Mystery.
We give thanks for all of who we are.
We give thanks for our places in the mysterious unfolding of all creation.
We ask that our hands be open and our hearts be pure
    so that our lives can be of service
        and, together with all beings, we will bring forth blessing.

פִּי יְדַבֵּר חָכְמוֹת וְהָגוּת לִבִּי תְבוּנוֹת

May my mouth speak wisdom,
    may the meditations of my heart bring forth understanding.

— Psalm 49:4

The Holy is revealed through us.

*... as the morning dawned there was thunder and lightning
and a thick cloud upon Mount Sinai. A loud blast of the shofar called,
and the people took their place at the foot of the mountain.*

— Exodus 19:16

*When God gave the Torah, no bird sang, no fowl flew, no ox bellowed,
no angel stirred a wing, the seraphim did not say Holy, Holy.
The sea did not roar, and no creature spoke.
The whole world stood hushed in breathless silence
and a voice went forth and proclaimed,
"I am the Mystery your God."*

— Exodus Rabbah 29:9

פָּנִים l בְּפָנִים דִּבֶּר יְהוָה עִמָּכֶם בָּהָר מִתּוֹךְ הָאֵשׁ

On the mountain, within the fire, the One spoke to us face within face.

— Deuteronomy 5:4

THE JOURNEY BEGAN the second night of Passover. Leaving *mitzrayim*, the narrow place, we set out to explore the wilderness. Seven weeks have passed and each of the 49 days have been woven into our souls. Everything that has happened has prepared us for this moment, this 50th day, when we stand together at Sinai.

Sinai is an experience of revelation, the tradition teaches. The Mystery speaks to each of us according to our strengths, according to our abilities. With thunder and lightning or in a still small voice, the Infinite breaks through and shows us something true.

Something we can live by.

We come to this 50th day and strive to say *Hineni*, Here I am. I have counted the days. I have walked the path. I am ready. I am open. I am willing to listen. And I am willing to take on *mitzvot*, actions, practices that will help cultivate my capacity to live in relationship with all life in honesty, love and grace.

Today we listen to a story our ancestors tell. We ask that it enter our souls and inspire our imagination and commitments.

It was before dawn on the fiftieth day.
  The air was cold and the sky deep blue
  When all of us awoke.

Together we walked slowly toward the mountain and stood.
  The ground trembled
  The mountain began to smoke.
  Lightening flashed. Thunder roared.
  A shofar called from the depths of the earth.
Then all was still.

Into the core of our being
    Within our heart, our soul, on the lines of our face
The One spoke
And everything vanished.
    There was no I, no you, no tree, no bird, no water, no fire.
    There was only One,
        One breath. Nothing more.
Only One.
    Forever. Eternal.
One.

Then the shofar wailed
    And the world in all its uniqueness rushed back
    Bird, wind, rock, sky
        And we stood with the One
        The breath still on our lips
            And we knew—
We knew
    The One inside the many
    The One beyond anything that can be known
And we trembled in awe
    We stepped back from the mountain
    We turned from the fire
        And we listened.
We listened to the One reverberate in our hearts

And in the silence, we heard these Ten Utterances:

I.   *I am, I was, I will be. I am the unfolding of all that is. I am constant*
      transformation calling you forward to be.

II.   *You cannot arrest me in motion. You cannot grasp or hold me.*
      Do not strive for certainty. Do not seek permanence.

III. *Do not use a Divine name to make false promises. Do not use*
      sacred teachings to lift up a destructive path.

IV. *Rest, Stop, Pause. Honor creation. Declare your freedom.*
      Rest and allow others to rest as well.

V. *Honor your parents. Honor your ancestors.*
    Honor those upon whose shoulders you stand.

VI. *Do not murder.*

VII. *Do not betray.*

VIII. *Do not steal.*

IX. *Do not use the power of words to hurt or destroy.*

X. *Feel the fullness of your life. Don't be led astray by comparing*
    yourself to others. Don't get lost in desiring what others have. Be content,
    be fulfilled with what your life brings.

Today, this 50ᵗʰ day,
We take upon ourselves *mitzvot.*
We take on practices to help us live with clarity and truth.

Take time today to reflect on the journey of these past 49 days.
Wonder about what you have encountered, what you have learned.
Make a commitment to a practice that will carry you forward.

Take on something you can do everyday that will keep you connected
    and awake. Listen and choose something that is true for you to do.
    Be wise and make a promise that feels possible to keep.
Carry this promise through the summer and into the fall.
On *Yom Kippur,* review your vow and how it has shaped your path.
    If the vow remains true, carry it with you. If it no longer serves, let
    it go into the light of *yom kippur.*

Shavuot, the 50ᵗʰ day, we renew our covenant with the One.
    We stand together with all life and say *Hineni.*
    Here I am. Ready, willing to enter into relationship.
    Ready and willing to be of service.
May my heart be open. May my intentions be clear.
May the work of my hands bring forth blessing and peace.

Listen, the Mystery calls, I am speaking
And I stand here as your witness.
 Do not bring me your bulls, your goats.
 Do not bring me the animals of your fields.
I know every bird of the mountain.
I know every creature of the forest, every sheep in the meadow,
They all belong to me.
 I fill the whole world.
 Creation flows through me.
 Do not offer what is already mine.

Listen, the Mystery calls,
It is the fiftieth day
And this is what I ask of you:
 Cultivate gratitude.
 Make a vow to live in relationship with all life.
 Ask for help in times of trouble and let yourself be guided.

Through this, the Mystery calls, you honor the One.
Through this, the Mystery calls,
 you bring the light of the Divine to dwell.
       — Psalm 50:7-15

WITH **D**EEP **G**RATITUDE to Carol Towarnicky, *editor*, and Bea Leopold, *graphic artist* and Phyllis Myers, *copy editor*. Their vision, insight, effort and love brought this Omer guide to be. Without them, it would have remained only a dream. I am so blessed by their trust and dedication to our shared vision. Thank you to Danielle Parmenter for her meticulous work in bringing forth the Hebrew Omer blessing.

Thank you to Beth Kaufman, Frida Samost and Norman Leopold for their beautiful photographs from Capitol Reef, Canyonlands and Zion National Parks in Utah and Ghost Ranch in New Mexico.

And to all those with whom I have counted the *Omer* over these many years, I am so grateful.

May it be for blessing.

— YL

Down from the Mountain

May our experiences of the Omer *and* Shavuot *continue to guide and shape the journey ahead. Here are six suggestions for practice in the coming weeks. If one or more speaks to you, we invite you to integrate it into your daily life. Use these pages to reflect on your experiences.*

OPENING THE DAY WITH GRATITUDE AND AWARENESS

Each morning as we arise, we say this prayer, letting it be the first words we utter upon awakening:

מוֹדה אני לפניך מלך חי וקים
שהחזרת בי נשְׁמתי בחמְלה רבה אמונתך

*Modeh/ Modah ani lefanecha melech chai vekayam,
she-he-chezarta bee nishmatee b'chemla, raba emunatecha*

I am grateful. I stand in relationship with the spirit of all life. You have returned my soul to me. Great is your faith in me.

PAUSING IN AWE AND WONDER

Once a day, as we eat something that comes from trees or the earth, we pause, examine its shape, color and texture, smell its fragrance and invite ourselves to wonder at the miracles of creation. Before eating, we say:

ברוך אתה יי אלהינו מלך העולם בורא פרי העץ (האדמה)

Baruch ata Yah elohaynu melech ha'olam borei pri ha'etz (ha'adamah)

Blessed are you Infinite One, our God, source of Mystery, who creates the fruit of the tree (of the earth).

BODY AND BREATH

As we begin our day, we take notice of the miracle of the breath moving through the body. We stand in an upright posture, stretch our arms, and bow if we are able. Standing, shoulders back, heart space open, say this prayer:

אלׄהי נשמה שנתת בי טהורה היא

Elohay neshamah shenatata bi tehorah he

The breath that fills all life is clear and true.

SHEMA

At the beginning of the day or when evening comes, we sit, take a few calming breaths and call out the *shema*. We pay attention as the words leave our lips and feel them resonate in our bodies:

שְׁמַע יִשְׂרָאֵל יְהוָה אֱלֹהֵינוּ יְהוָה אֶחָד

Shema ysrael, Yah elohaynu, Yah echad

Listen, pay attention: the Infinite Unfolding, in all its diversity, the Infinite Unfolding is One.

EVENING GRATITUDE

As we end our day, we reflect upon our encounters and give voice to two experiences for which we feel grateful. Then we say

מַה־גָּדְלוּ מַעֲשֶׂיךָ יְהוָה מְאֹד עָמְקוּ מַחְשְׁבֹתֶיךָ

Mah gadlu ma'asecha Yah m'od amku mach'sh'votecha
How great is the unfolding of all life, how deep the mystery.

— Psalm 92:6

EVENING FORGIVENESS

As we end the day we say this prayer:

Guide of the Universe, I forgive anyone who angered, antagonized or hurt me today, whether he or she did so accidentally or willfully, whether through speech or deed.

May I be forgiven for any wrongs I have done today through action or word, willfully or by accident. May compassion and kindness be my guide.

יִהְיוּ לְרָצוֹן ׀ אִמְרֵי־פִי וְהֶגְיוֹן לִבִּי לְפָנֶיךָ יְהֹוָה צוּרִי וְגֹאֲלִי

May the words of my mouth,
the meditations of my heart,
and the work of my hands,
be aligned with the Highest Will.
May the Mystery hold me steady and call me forth.

— Psalm 19:15

Notes

Made in the USA
Middletown, DE
09 August 2017